POEMS

گزیدهٔ شعر

Shakila Azizzada

POEMS

گزیدۀ شعر

First published in 2012
by The Poetry Translation Centre Ltd
PO Box 61051
London SE16 4YY

www.poetrytranslation.org

Poems © Shakila Azizzada, 2012

Translations from the Dari © Mimi Khalvati and Zuzanna Olszewska
Introduction © Zuzanna Olszewska

ISBN: 978-0-9560576-7-9

The Poetry Translation Centre gratefully acknowledges the financial support
of Arts Council England.

British Library Cataloguing-in-Publication Data.
A catalogue record for this book is available from the British Library.

Designed in Albertina by Libanus Press
Printed in the UK by Imprint Digital

Contents

Introduction	7
Haft Seen	11
Signs of God	13
Cat Lying in Wait	15
A Feather	19
The Tryst	21
Once Upon a Time	23
Epitaph	27
Recitation	29
Kabul	33

Introduction

Shakila Azizzada is a unique voice in Afghan poetry, situated at the confluence of the Persian and Western poetic traditions. Born in Kabul in 1964, she fled war and occupation and settled in the Netherlands, where she has now spent more than half her life, at the age of 20. She is thus proficient enough in Persian (Dari) and Dutch to write poetry in both languages – an ability she considers a blessing – and both cultures have left an imprint on her poetic style and themes.

Azizzada was born into a cultured family which held the classics of Persian literature – Hafez, Ferdowsi's *Book of Kings*, and Bidel – in customary high esteem. Her older brother, a journalist, nurtured her young talent by introducing her to important modernist poets such as the Iranians Nima Yushij and Forough Farrokhzad. He encouraged her to go beyond the short stories she wrote for a children's magazine in her teens and try her hand at poetry. Her early work, like much literature in Afghanistan at the time, was political, and she started out in rhyming and metric classical forms, but soon found that she could express herself much more freely in blank verse. She left Afghanistan after completing a degree in law; later, in the Netherlands, she studied oriental languages and literatures at the University of Utrecht. Her first collection of poetry, *Herinnering aan niets* (*Memories about Nothing*), was published in 2004 in separate Persian and Dutch editions. The poems in this volume have been selected from that book and from her forthcoming second collection.

Azizzada's work is unusual in Afghan poetry in Persian (Dari) for the intimacy and individuality of its expression. She renders her own emotional landscapes with the patience and precision of a miniature painter, and strives to do the same for others whose inner worlds she imaginatively enters. She invites us to share tender instants with her, such as her young daughter slipping into her bed to fall asleep in her arms ('A Feather'), or her nostalgia for stolen moments shared in youth with a former sweetheart she may never see again ('The Tryst'). More daring for an Afghan woman are her confessional poems on the subject of sexual desire, such as the magnetism of a seduction against one's better judgement in 'Cat Lying in Wait'. Here we detect a greater kinship with the Western poets she admires – Octavio Paz, Anne Sexton and Sylvia Plath – than with the conventions of Persian love poetry and their many-layered, metaphorical evasiveness.

And yet, both Azizzada's Afghan origins and the indelible mark of the tragedies her people have faced are evident in her poetry. In 'Epitaph' she evokes, almost tauntingly, the human frailty of a typical *mujahed* (one of the commanders of the anti-Soviet resistance who later fought each other in Afghanistan's civil wars): as a warrior who will live and die by the gun, and as a man who is also a son and a lover. 'Once Upon a Time' is a lament for a friend, herself a writer, who lost her whole family in the wars and in exile, told as an improvisation on an old Afghan fairy tale about a quest and a sack filled with magical objects. 'Recitation' and 'Yalda' are Azizzada's tributes to Afghan girls killed in war or abused by their own families. Meanwhile, in 'Haft Seen' she confronts both the nostalgia and the resilience of the exile, laying out her Persian New Year spread in Amsterdam's Dam Platz with no-one but the pigeons for company. Difficult to translate, but evident in the Dari originals, is frequent word play and use of evocative colloquial phrases.

This selection ends with a haunting, surreal elegy for a Kabul whose human and material fabric has disintegrated: a Kabul that

English-speakers rarely see described through the eyes of one of its former inhabitants in her own idiom. We hope these translations provide an insight into that world, and into Shakila Azizzada's meditations on love and loss – and the quiet but insistent determination to start over and shape her own life.

ZUZANNA OLSZEWSKA

هفت سین

ابری اگر نبود
می توانستی
از این آسمان کوتاه
دانه دانه
ستاره بچینی،
از موهای مدام آشفته اش
بیاویزی
و انگار کنی
می گوید:

به قالین َموْر می مانم
که هرچه کهنه شود
زیباتر می گردد
هرچند
دو، سه بچه ی شیطان
بر آن شاشیده باشد

رسیدی؟

حالا سفره ی هفت سین را
میان میدان "دام" پهن کن

باران هم که ببارد
سپاهی گم نام
با خیل کبوتران
مهمان تواند

HAFT SEEN

If it weren't for the clouds,
I could
pick the stars
one by one
from this brief sky,
hang them
in your ever ruffled hair
and hear
you saying:

'I'm like a silk rug –
the older it gets,
the lovelier it grows,
even if
two or three naughty kids
did pee on it.'

Am I finally here?

Then let me spread
the Haft Seen tablecloth
in the middle of Dam Platz.

Even if it rains,
The Unknown Soldier
and a flock of pigeons
will be my guests.

Haft Seen: traditional display of seven symbolic items beginning with the letter 's', prepared for the New Year festival of Now Ruz.

Dam Platz: historical square in Amsterdam flanked by the Royal Palace and the National Memorial to the Dutch war dead.

نشانه های خدا

در دل اُرسی قاب می شوی

بر سر انگشتانت
گرمی شانه هایش می ماسد

باران
رد پا هایش را
زیر فانوس کوچه می شوید

از لای دفتر بسته
خیال او
به شب های رفته می کوچد

آن طرف تر
سایه ی گربه ی شبگرد را گم می کنی

به بیت اول بسنده
کلام حافظ را
بر طاقچه اُرسی می گذاری

بر دستمال ابریشمی
که کتاب مادر را
گوش تا گوش در خود پیچانده است،
دست می کشی

به ریتم متن نخوانده
شانه هایت
زیر شال نقره ای می لرزند

نشانه های خدا
درون قامت اوراد کهنه می پوسند

SIGNS OF GOD

You are framed in the heart of a window.

The warmth of his shoulders
hardens on your fingertips.

Under the streetlamps,
rain washes away his footprints.

Your notebook's closed
but the thought of him slips out
to rejoin the nights now gone.

And over there, the shadow of a cat,
night-wandering too, is lost.

Since the first verse will do,
you put Hafez
back on the windowsill.

You run your hand
over the silk handkerchief,
knotted corner to corner,
the Mother Book is wrapped in.

Under a silver shawl,
your shoulders, in silent
rhythm to the texts, are shaking.

Inside the covers of the old verses,
signs of God are rotting.

The Mother Book: the Koran

کمین گربه

شگوم ندارد
این واژه ها

نگو در بهشت
میان لب های من باز می شود

پای خدا
در چاک سینه های من لغزیده است

می آیم

باز
نفس هایت
درمن می دمند
ریه هایت
از عطر من پر می شوند
زبانت بر پوستم
باران باران
بارانی می شود

وا می روم

و باز
آنگونه که می آیی
با هوای دریدن
در نی نی چشم هایت

بی هیچ شکی

CAT LYING IN WAIT

They don't bode well,
these words.

Don't tell me the door to Paradise
opens between my lips.

In the cleft between my breasts,
God himself tripped.

I'll come

and again
your breath will breathe
inside me,
your lungs will fill
with my scent,
your tongue will
rain, rain,
rain again on my skin.

I'll give in.

And this time,
when you come with that glint
in your eye, bent
on tearing me apart, you'll be,

without a shadow of a doubt,

به گربه‌ی سیاه می مانی
که پیشترک
از کمینگاهش
راه را بر من برید
تا دم درت
گنجشک فلج شده
از تسلیم را
شکار کرده باشد

like the black cat that leapt
out of hiding, cut
across my path just now,
hunted down
the sparrow at your door
till she fell
stunned and captive.

پَر

آرام، آرام می آیی
بر نوک پاها
درست وقتی رویا
صدای پایت را می شنود

چشم هایت خمار مانند
وقتی گربه وار
زیر لحافم می خزی
خواب و بیدار
حریر خوابم را می بوسی

در فاصله ی رساندن دست هایت
به دور گردنم
روی بالش من به خواب می روی

میان خواب و بیداری
به محض خالی شدن از رویا
پُر می شوم از تو

A FEATHER
for Sapieda

Just as my dream
hears the sound of your steps,
that's when you enter
quietly, quietly on tiptoe.

You crawl under the sheet
like a kitten, your eyes
drinking me in.
Asleep or awake,
you lap the silk of my dreams.

In the moment it takes
to put your arms round my neck,
you're fast asleep on the pillow.

And I, half-asleep, half-awake,
just when I am drained of dream,
am filled with you and replenished.

دیدار

سال هاست
که دیدار
دیگر نه به قسمت
به قیامت است

دلداری می کنی

می گویی
جوراب سیاه اسب نشان
بر پاهای تو
زیبا بود

هوس می کنم
نگاهت
یک بار هم شده
از پرپر زدن بیفتد
و باز
بر بند کفش هایم
میخکوب شود

تخت است یا تابوت؟

زیرنسترن لب جوی

هزار پهلو
پیش تر از بیداری شاید

با تو
در رویایی
دیدار تازه می کنم
که از پرواز زنبوری
به دور اناری ترکیده
پریشان شده بود

THE TRYST

It's been years since we could say
'with luck, we'll meet again',
since now we know for certain
we'll only meet on Judgement Day.

I know you'd cheer me up.

You'd tell me,
'those black school tights
looked gorgeous on your legs.'

If only, just for once,
I could see
your shy glance
stop fluttering and fall
and be riveted
once more
on my laces.

Heads or tails?

Before waking from a night
of tossing and turning, maybe

I'll meet you again
under the wings
of a rambling rose by a stream
in a dream broken
by the buzzing of a bee
round a pomegranate,
split open.

بود، نبود

ننه می گفت
توبره را
بر صندوق سینه نگه دار

نگو آفتاب کهنه شده
نگو بیگاه شد
بگو باز می آیم

دیو سپید
پشت و پناهت باشد

های،
دختر پگاه!
سستی کار
شاید از دست های توست
که افسانه هم
پای در گِل مانده است

شانه را
از توبره بیرون آر
سر راه بدخواه
پرتاب کن
تا هفت جنگل
در پیش پاهایش بروید

نگو آسمان دور
زمین سخت است

از دریا و پری هایش
اگر می ترسی
آیینه را
پرتاب نکن

ONCE UPON A TIME
in memory of Leila Sarahat Roshani

Granny used to say
always keep your magic sack
tucked inside your ribcage.

Don't say the sun's worn out,
don't say it's gone astray.
Say, I'm coming back.

May the White Demon
protect and watch over you.
Oh, daughter of the dawn,

perhaps this sorry tale,
stuck in the mud,
was of your own doing.

Take the comb from the sack,
throw it in the Black Demon's path:
seven jungles will grow at his feet.

Don't say heaven's too far,
earth's too hard. Don't throw the mirror
if you fear the sea and her nymphs.

Don't say there was, don't say there wasn't,
trust in the god of fairytales.
May Granny's soul rest in peace.

نگو نبود
به خدای افسانه ها بسپار
ننه را بیامرزد

آیینه را
به دست مادر گلنار بده
که پیش پای تاکستان های سوخته
خواب مرغ و ماهی می بیند

نگو آفتاب لب بام
کوتاه است

بگو می آیم
و این بار
دل صاحب مرده ات را
جمع کن

توبره را بتکان
به نام دیو سپید
آن تار موی را
دود کن

مگر نبود؟

بود نبود
دختری بود
که در خواب های دیر و مدامش
زنی پیچه سپید
پیوسته ورد میخواند:

شمالی هنوز
سرشار ترانه است
و از چت خانه های ویرانش
روشنی می بارد

Give the mirror to Golnar's mother
who, down by the charred vineyards,
dreams of birds and fish.

Don't say the rooftop sun's too brief.
Say, I'm coming and this time,
forget love's foolish griefs.

Shake out the sack.
In the name of the White Demon,
burn that strand of hair.

Wasn't there,
once upon a time . . . ?
Once upon a time there was

a girl in whose long, endless dreams,
an old woman with white braids,
forever telling beads, would pray:

'May the Shomali Plain still fill with song
and through the ceilings
of its ruined homes, let light pour in.'

Once Upon a Time: this poem refers to a fairytale in which the hero sets off to fight the Black Demon, aided by the White Demon and the magic powers of a sack with a mirror, a comb and a strand of hair. Fairytales traditionally start with the refrain, 'There was one, there wasn't one, apart from God, there was no one'.

لوح

در چشمان میشی ات
آخرین نفسِ
کدام ها می خوابد؟

نگاه کدام کودک
با ماشه ات خالی می شود؟

دلت برای کدام دوشیزه ی
دل در کفِ
پای در خون می تپد؟

کوه مرد!
کدام تقدیر
صخره از زیر پا هایت می گیرد؟

سیاه زلفان به خاک آلوده ات
نوک پستان های کدام زن را می سوزاند؟

بگو
نفس آخر تو
ته چشمان که آرام می گیرد؟

EPITAPH

Whose dying breaths
are sleeping
in your hazel eyes?

What small child's gaze
goes blank at your trigger?

For what young girl,
    her heart in your palm,
        legs bloodied, does your heart beat?

Mountain man!
What fate will tear the cliffs
from under your feet?

What woman will feel her nipples burn
for your black curls in the dust,
what mother for her son?

Tell me,
in the depths of whose eyes
will your dying breaths find peace?

What woman will feel her nipples burn: refers to a saying among the mothers of men killed on the battlefield in Afghanistan who felt their nipples burning when their sons were killed.

واگویه

در گلوی مادر
"نازی" با هزار ناز
زنده زنده می سوزد

سینه سوراخ هم که باشد
صندوقچه ی هزار ناز نهفته است

"لا ااااااااا اله"
بیراه می رود قاری
کُرت نازبو
در هوا منتشر می شود
و "لااله" در دهان قاری می ماسد

انگشتان مادر
گیسوان آشفته را
تار تار
پس گوش دختر می خواباند

بر زانوانش
سر و گردن وارفته
یک دامن گل می شود

دست ها در هوا
گاه بر فرق سر
"نازی" می موید مادر
و در لای انگشت هایش
غُمچه غُمچه مو های جو گندمی می روید

RECITATION

Her name, Nazaneen, along
with a thousand other caresses,
burns in her mother's throat
like a flame, a flame.

Her chest may be pierced
but it's a treasure chest
of a thousand hidden endearments.

Laaa ellah! The mullah
has strayed from the path.
A bed of sweet basil is spreading
its scent through the air and
La ella! . . . his oath stops short.

Her mother's fingers
are smoothing her tangled curls
back behind her ears,
strand by strand.

Propped on her mother's knee,
her head and neck, lying limp,
meld into a lap of flowers.

Nazaneen! her mother wails,
throwing her hands up, hitting
her head as, clump by torn-out clump,
white hairs like wheat and barley
sprout between her fingers.

ملافه ی سپید می سُرد
در زخم سینه و پستان های نورس عریان
داغ دل مادر واگویه می شود

"لاله" می گوید قاری

اسپندی
سرش می چرخد

بوی کافور
با اوراد مادر می آمیزد
نیست
خدایی
نیست
خدایی
نیست
خدایی
نیست

The white sheet slips.
The chest wound, the girlish breasts
laid bare, renew her mother's anguish.

La ellah! says the mullah.

The incense-thrower
turns her head.
The scent of camphor
mingles with the mother's plaints:
There is
no God,
there is
no God,
there is
no God,
no God.

Recitation: this poem alludes to the many girls killed during the civil war in Kabul, 1992–1996.

La ellah!: suggesting annoyance, an abbreviation of *La ilaha illa Allah wa Muhammad rasoul Allah*, 'There is no God but God and Muhammad His Prophet'. Those who use the abbreviation, 'There is no God' are unintentionally blasphemous, though the mother here uses it literally.

کابل

برای کابل
اگر دلم می تپد
برای دامن بالاحصار است
که مرده هایم را
در آغوش می کشد

هر چند، هیچ گاه
هیچ یک از آن دل های نامراد
برای من نتپیده است

برای کابل
اگر دلم می سوزد
برای "ویش خدا" گفتن لیلا است
که دل مادر کلان را
کلچه کلچه داغ می زد

برای راه کشیدن چشم های گلنار است
که از پگاه تا بیگاه
از بهار تا تیر ماه
آنقدر بر راه ماندند
تا همه ی جاده ها پوسیدند
و بیراهه هایش
ناگهان
در خواب های نورس من
پوست انداختند

برای کابل
اگر دلم می لرزد
برای نیمروز های کند پای تابستان است
که هنوز خانه ی پدری را
به سنگینی خواب نیم چاشتی اش
بر صندوق سینه ام بار می کند

KABUL

If my heart beats
for Kabul,
it's for the slopes of Bala Hissar,
holding my dead
in its foothills.

Though not one, not one
of those wretched hearts
ever beat for me.

If my heart grieves
for Kabul,
it's for Leyla's sighs of
'Oh, dear God!'
and my grandmother's heart
set pounding.

It's for Golnar's eyes
scanning the paths
from dawn to dusk, spring to autumn,
staring so long
that all the roads fall apart
and in my teenage nightmares
side roads
suddenly shed their skins.

If my heart trembles
for Kabul,
it's for the slow step of summer noons,
siestas in my father's house which,
heavy with mid-day sleep,
still weighs on my ribs.

برای فرشته ی بازیگوش شانه ی راست
که هی یادش می رود
گلوله های غیبی را بتاراند

برای گم شدن صدای
سبزی فروش دوره گرد
در خواب های پریشان همسایه هاست
که دلم می لرزد

For the playful Angel of the Right Shoulder
who keeps forgetting
to ward away stray bullets.

It's for the hawker's cry
of the vegetable seller doing his rounds,
lost in my neighbours' troubled dreams,
that my heart's trembling.

Bala Hissar: an ancient citadel in Kabul with a cemetery outside its walls.

Angel of the Right Shoulder: one of the angelic *Keraman Katebin*, who sit on the shoulders of believers, recording their good and evil deeds.